# ORIGIN OF THE PEOPLE OF INDIA AND THE VEDIC CULTURE

Fifth Edition

Linga Raju, M. D.

Origin of the People of India and the Vedic Culture

Fifth Edition

This fifth edition soft cover book has been slightly modified from the original fifth edition book with the same ISBN: 9781717850232

December 2020

# Contents

Introduction ............................................................. 5

Climate Change Patterns ........................................ 8

Sea Levels ............................................................. 12

Stone Tools .......................................................... 14

Dating Methods .................................................... 17

Deoxyribonucleic acid .......................................... 18

Mitochondrial DNA ............................................... 18

Nuclear DNA ........................................................ 20

The ancestors of humans ..................................... 21

The Humans ......................................................... 23

Anatomically Modern Humans ............................. 27

Route of migration out of Africa .......................... 30

The great exodus ................................................. 34

The Genetic Studies ............................................. 37

Mitochondrial DNA studies .................................. 38

Non-recombinant Y-chromosomal DNA studies .... 42

One Family ........................................................... 56

The Theory of Aryan Invasion of India is a Fallacy
............................................................................. 57

Ārya ...................................................................... 70

Archaeological Findings of the Vedic Civilization .. 75

Timing of the Vedic Civilization ........................... 83

The Sacred Hindu Scriptures ................................... 88

Veda ............................................................................. 90

Chanting the Veda ................................................. 100

Sanskrit Script ........................................................ 104

References ............................................................. 108

# INTRODUCTION

The readers may very well know this, but right at the outset it is to be pointed out that the term *'human'* refers to all the species of the genera *'Homo'*, and that *'anatomically modern human'* applies only to the species *'Homo sapiens'*.

*'As soon as he was born, he spread eastward and westward over the Earth'* says Rigveda X.90.5 (reference 1). It seems that that is what has happened.

About 200,000 years ago the anatomically modern humans originated in the east-central part of the African continent. From there they spread eastward out of Africa, and westward in the African continent. There is no evidence that there were any different parallel evolutionary origins of the anatomically modern humans in India or anywhere else other than in Africa.

The first migration out of Africa by the anatomically modern humans was about 120,000 years ago. The first migrants out of Africa made it into the Levant, but they died out there. The Levant is a narrow corridor by the sea between the Mediterranean Sea to the north-west and deserts to the south-east. It is mainly the present day Syria and the surrounding regions.

The second migration out of Africa by the anatomically modern humans was about 85,000 years ago. All non-African people including the people of India are the descendants of this group of modern humans who exited Africa about 85,000 years ago. In a sense, all the people of the world are part of one family.

Anatomically modern humans had already arrived in India by 75,000 year ago. India has emerged as the oldest continuous civilization on earth. New biological evidence suggests that the Indian population has lived in the peninsula for at least the past 75,000 years.

In order to better understand the origin of the people of India, it is prudent to review the evolution of humans in general.

Climate change patterns such as repeated glacial cycles have been helpful in determining when in time and where in place the human migration movements have occurred.

Paleo-anthropologic studies of ancestors including the analysis of skull shapes have resulted in better understanding of the evolution of the human.

Newer approaches to dating techniques have given information about the ancestors going back millions of years.

More importantly, advances in deoxyribonucleic acid (DNA) analysis techniques have been of tremendous help in understanding the evolution and migration of the anatomically modern humans.

Thus, all these topics are to be reviewed to better understand the origin of the people of India.

## CLIMATE CHANGE PATTERNS

Climate change is a change in the weather patterns when that change lasts for an extended period of time – lasting decades to millions of years. Fluctuations over periods shorter than a few decades, such as El Nino, do not represent climate change.

The weather patterns are caused by the differences between the rate at which energy is received from the Sun and the rate at which it is lost to space. The mechanisms involved are the variations in the solar radiation, variations in the Earth's orbit such as variations in Earth's eccentricity, changes in the tilt angle of Earth's axis of rotation, and precession of Earth's axis, variation in reflectivity of continents and oceans, mountain-building and continental drift, and changes in greenhouse gas concentration. The energy is distributed around the globe by winds, ocean currents, and other mechanisms to affect the climate of different regions (wikipedia.org).

There seems to be enough evidence to suggest that certain human activities may contribute to ongoing climate change referred to as the global warming.

**Ice age** is a period of long term reduction in the temperature of Earth's surface and atmosphere, resulting in expansion of continental and polar ice sheets and alpine glaciers.

Within a long term ice age, individual periods of cold climate are termed *'glacial period' or 'glaciations'*. The glacial period is an interval of time (thousands of years) within an ice age that is marked by colder temperatures and glacial advances. Further, within a long term ice age an intermediate warm period is called the *'interglacial period'*. Interglacial is a period of warmer climate between glacial periods. **The present time is said to be an interglacial period within a long term ice age** (wikipedia.org).

Understanding the climate change pattern is an important process in determining the effects of repeated glaciations on evolution and migration. Repeated and intense cold seasons result in glaciations, and the worst ones cause widespread extinctions.

Historical climate change record is based on geological evidences obtained from borehole temperature profiles, cores removed from deep accumulations of ice, floral and faunal records, glacial processes, stable-isotope and other analyses of sediment layers, records of past sea levels, and such (wikipedia.org).

Some examples of obtaining such climate change information are - drilling into ice-caps such as in Greenland, drilling seabeds particularly of the Arabian Sea and at various locations of the Indian Ocean, and digging the ground in various places.

Extreme cold weather brings *glaciations of ice ages*. During these glacial periods, large volumes of water are held in ice-sheets which may be as thick as a mile. The sea levels fall. There is less evaporation from the oceans, there is less rain, and the desert belts expand over large territories of land.

Extreme glaciations, called *glacial maximum*, are rare and short lived. They have occurred twice over the past 200,000 years. The 'Last Glacial Maximum' was about 25,000 years ago, the deglaciation started about 18,000-17,000 BCE.

Brief episodes of warming are also rare. Very warm period called *'Interglacial Optimum'* has occurred most recently about 8,000 years ago. The global sea levels rose, and they were 8 to 13 feet above the twentieth century average. During these warm periods, lush greenery expands, and grasslands and lakes grow into the deserts. A warm spell that lasts only a few thousand years, is called an interstadial rather than an interglacial.

**Most of the immediate past two and a half million year period has been an extended cold and icy period, with only brief periods of warming.**

A climatic catastrophe of some importance occurred about 74,000 years ago. According to potassium-argon dating, the Toba super volcanic eruption occurred 75,000+or-900 years ago (wikipedia.org). The volcanic eruption of Toba in Sumatra was the biggest eruption of the last two million years. A huge plume of ash spread north-west and covered a wide area, particularly India. It caused prolonged winter lasting about 1,000 years, and deposited an ash layer of 3 to 10 feet deep.

Another incident of historical interest occurred about 66 million years ago. There was about 30,000 years of volcanic activity from the Deccan Traps in India (wikipedia.org).

## SEA LEVELS

Mean Sea Level is an average level of the surface of one or more of Earth's oceans. The sea level can be affected by many factors. The sea is in constant motion affected by the tides, wind, atmospheric pressure, local gravitational differences, temperature, salinity, and so forth (wikipedia.org).

Sea level can be determined by averaging the hourly observations made over a period of one or more years. Since the year 1992 satellite altimeters have been making precise measurements of sea level. The sea level has risen by about 200 millimeters or 7.9 inches (2 mm/year) during the twentieth century (wikipedia.org).

Retrospectively determining the prehistoric sea levels is not easy. In the ice ages, the main cause of sea level variations was the formation or melting of continental glaciers.

The interglacial high sea levels are determined by looking at coral reefs. But, it is more difficult to determine the low sea levels during glaciations. This information is obtained by measuring prehistoric levels of Red Sea plankton.

When sea levels are very low, the Red Sea effectively becomes a salt lake with very little exchange from the Indian Ocean. Evaporation of water increases the salinity of water, and this kills plankton which is the base of marine food chain. When sea levels improve, water exchange between the Red Sea and Indian Ocean restores plankton in the Red Sea (reference 2). By measuring the historic levels of Red Sea plankton, low sea levels can be determined retrospectively.

## STONE TOOLS

Stone has been used to make a wide variety of different tools over the years. Prehistoric period during which stone was used to make tools has been called the **'Stone Age'**. The Stone Age is said to have lasted about 3.4 million years, ending between 8,700 Before Common Era (BCE) and 2,000 BCE (wikipedia.org).

Stone has been fashioned to make implements with an edge, a point, or a percussion surface. Abundant information has been obtained by the study of stone tools.

The stone-tool technologies have been classified as - Lower, Middle and Upper Paleolithic, Mesolithic, and Neolithic.

Lower Paleolithic also called Earlier/Early Stone Age, started around 2.6 million years ago, or may be as far back as 3.4 million ears ago.

The Middle Paleolithic also called Middle Stone Age was from about 300,000 to 50,000 years ago.

The Upper Paleolithic also called The Later Stone Age, is from about 50,000 to 10,000 years ago.

The Mesolithic was from about 10,000 to 6,000 years ago.

The Neolithic started around 7,000 Before Common Era (BCE).

Transition from the Stone Age to the Age of the Metals occurred between 6,000 BCE and 2,500 BCE.

**The chronology of these stone ages is not absolute.** As advances were made, the older technology was not discarded. The progress was cumulative.

### Stone artifacts in India

**India is rich in stone artifacts.** The older Lower Paleolithic tools called Acheulian tools date roughly from 670,000 to 160,000 years ago, while the newer Middle Paleolithic tools appear at the end of that period around 160,000 years ago. Abundant Middle Paleolithic stone tools found in India are probably made by late pre-modern or archaic humans who were there in India at the time. Modern humans were not yet there in India at that time (2).

The earliest evidence of deliberate patterning of stone that had some symbolic purpose – regular scratches, cross-hatching, and notching of pieces of stone or mineral pigment blocks – dating to 300,000 to 150,000 years ago have been found in the sandstone caves of India (2).

The change from Middle Paleolithic to the Upper Paleolithic stone tools is also seen in the Central Narmada and in the Middle Son Basin in India. This is said to have been associated with a volcanic ash layer from the Toba super volcanic eruption that occurred about 74,000 years ago. (2). The Upper Paleolithic tools were made by the anatomically modern humans who had already arrived there in India. The modern humans who survived did not arrive in Levant and Europe until much later (2). The Levant is a narrow corridor by the sea between the Mediterranean Sea to the north-west and deserts to the south-east. It is mainly the present day Syria and the surrounding regions.

## DATING METHODS

Dating of an artifact can be accomplished by a direct study of the artifact, or by the study of the materials found in association with the artifact at the point of discovery.

Carbon dating of the artifact has a limited capability of going back only up to 40,000 years or so. But Uranium dating can take it much further back. For example the Uranium-Thorium dating has an upper limit of over 500,000 years or so. And the newer approaches of luminescence dating of silica and such can go much beyond.

All these advances mentioned in the articles given above have given information about the ancestors going back millions of years. Furthermore, they have helped resolve some of the past 200,000 year family tree issues associated with the deoxyribonucleic acid (DNA) analysis.

## DEOXYRIBONUCLEIC ACID

Every cell in our body has deoxyribonucleic acid (**DNA**) in two places – in the nucleus and in the mitochondria. Most of the DNA is inside the nucleus of the cell. Only a very small portion of DNA is outside the nucleus in the mitochondria which are located in the cytoplasm of the cells.

Deoxyribonucleic acid collects mutations over time, and is inherited. Thus, it contains historical information. Evolutionary history can be obtained by comparing the DNA sequences.

## MITOCHONDRIAL DNA

Mitochondria are the power houses located in the cytoplasm of the cell.

The mitochondrial DNA is inherited only from the mother. Although it is inherited by both the daughters and the sons, only the daughters can transmit it further to the next generation. Both ovum and sperm have mitochondria, but the sperm's mitochondria wither out upon entry into the ovum, and only the ovum's mitochondria are transmitted.

The mitochondrial DNA is not corrupted by intermixing with other DNA during transmission from one generation to the next. But, during this generational transmission of the mitochondrial DNA, a random mutation called a DNA point mutation occurs every one thousand generations or so (2).

Over the past 200,000 years a number of mutations on the mitochondrial DNA have accumulated and have been passed down to the daughters. This may represent about seven to fifteen mutations in each person, but it becomes more complicated when dealing with the people of the whole world with thousands of combinations of mutations (2).

The random mutations that have occurred on different mitochondrial DNA of mothers in different places around the world have been passed down to respective daughters. These different combinations of mutations in the present day living women around the world have been determined, and have been used to reconstruct a female family tree that can be traced backwards to the first mothers about 200,000 years ago. This family tree gives information as to not only in which part of the world a particular mutation has occurred but also when in time it occurred. All this information has helped trace the migration of modern humans around the world.

## NUCLEAR DNA

The nuclear DNA is inherited from both parents. During reproduction, the parents' nuclear DNA is copied and transmitted in equal portions. Although the nuclear DNA is segregated during reproduction, small bits of the DNA are shuffled and mixed at each generation. This is known as recombination. However, part of the Y-chromosome does not participate in this recombination process. The non-recombining part of the Y-chromosome gives uncorrupted information that is transmitted from generation to generation.

### Non-recombining Y-chromosome DNA

Y-chromosome is the male chromosome that is transmitted from father to son only. The non-recombining Y-chromosome DNA is much larger in size than the tiny mitochondrial DNA. Therefore, it may have a greater power of time and geographic resolution than the mitochondrial DNA. But it gives a wider range of estimated time periods.

The Y-chromosomal study has helped chart a male genetic trail similar to the female one of the mitochondrial DNA (2).

## THE ANCESTORS OF HUMANS

About ten million years ago Africa was a lush place with open forests and home to several ape species. Separation of the ancestors of humans from the orangutans is said to have taken place between 10 and 20 million years ago. Then, separation from the gorillas was about 9 million years ago.

Around 7 to 8 million years ago, a dramatic reduction in the number of ape species coincided with several million years of global cooling. And about 6.5 million years ago there was a branching off in the evolutionary tree, separating the ancestors of humans from the ancestors of chimpanzees.

*Australopithecus anamnesis* skeletons dating from 4 million years ago, found on the shores of Lake Turkana in northern Kenya in Africa, were bipedal – the walking ape ancestors of humans. The most important initial physical change in the ancestors was walking on two legs.

Partial skeleton of the famous *Lucy* was discovered in 1974 at Hadar in the Afar Triangle region of northern Ethiopia in Africa. This Lucy family, *Australopithecus afarensis*, is dated to be 3 to 4 million years old. Lucy was about 40 to 60 inches tall, upright and bipedal with a pelvis and leg bones more similar to that of humans, but the skull size and the cranial cavity size (brain size) were small similar to those of the chimpanzees.

A jaw-bone fossil dated to be about 2.8 million years old, discovered in 2015 in Ethiopia, Africa, is said to represent an intermediate stage between Australopithecus and the genus Homo, the humans (wikipedia.org).

## THE HUMANS

*'Human'* refers to all the species of the genera *'Homo'*. It was previously thought that about 2.5 million years ago the first humans appeared in the African savannah, and then spread out of Africa. The previous earliest finding of the genus Homo was at Dmanisi in Georgia dating to 1.85 million years ago. But the recent findings of human artifacts in the Siwalk Hills north of New Delhi, India, dating back to at least 2.6 million years ago, suggests that humans may have left Africa half a million years earlier than previously thought (wikipedia.org).

The most salient development in the humans was an increase in the cranial capacity (brain size) from about 450 cubic centimeters in *Australopithecus garhi* to about 600 cubic centimeters in *Homo habilis* (wikipedia.org).

By one million years ago, the brain volume of various human species had increased to about 1,000 cubic centimeters which is about three-quarters of the modern volume, and the humans had spread out outside Africa.

The *Homo erectus* species dominated the earth for a million and a half years. Slightly smaller than the modern human, *Homo erectus* rapidly spread from Africa to the Middle East, India, Southeast Asia, Russia and the Far East. There is no evidence that they migrated to the Americas.

They had relatively large brains and used stone tools. First the simple stone tools were re-touched pebbles, and later the tools were more sophisticated like the hand axes.

There was a series of ice age glaciations over a million years ago drying up Africa. Then another specialized species of humans *Homo rhodesiensis* arose. They had the same size body as modern humans, and the cranial cavity size (brain volume) of as much as 1,250 cubic centimeters. They used Lower Paleolithic tools – flat stones shaped on both sides to form tear-drop shaped pointed hand-axes. During a brief warm period about 500,000 years ago, they made it out of Africa to Europe with their tools, and later became *Homo heidelbergensis*.

About 350,000 years ago, there was another severe glaciation of ice age. Subsequently about 300,000 years ago, *archaic human species Homo helmei* evolved. Their brain volume was actually larger than that of modern humans at about 1,400 cubic centimeters. They had developed the Middle Paleolithic tool technology. During a warm period around 250,000 years ago, many of them had moved out of Africa and spread throughout Europe and Asia.

**The Valley of Narmada River in central India was home to a large brained archaic human** (2).

The archaic human species *Homo helmei* seems to have given rise to *Homo neanderthalensis* species. The Neanderthals also had a similarly larger brain than modern humans and used Middle Paleolithic tools. They were in Europe and Asia including India and China. **There were no Neanderthals in Africa.**

The increase in evolutionary brain volume in the ancestors of humans as compared to the ancestors of chimpanzees seems to correlate with quantitative differences in the increase in intellectual ability. **The only qualitative difference between humans and the chimpanzees is the human speech.** Speech-driven co-evolution in brain size has been remarkable. Recent genome studies reveal that Humans and the late Neanderthals share the FOXP2 gene variant associated with speech and brain development, whereas the Chimpanzees have two amino acid differences in that gene (Wikipedia.org).

It seems that every time there is a drastic climate change, there is an evolutionary change, and a migratory movement.

Climate and geography dictate where to go and where to stay/live. The dictates are: While going, avoid deserts and high mountains, and follow the rivers and the game. When staying, stay near water and vegetation and near reliable rainfall. All the migratory movements seem to have happened this way.

In an entirely different context, the connection between all beings, the earth, water, vegetation and human speech, is mentioned in the Chandogya Upanishad, chapter I, verse 2 (reference 3). It goes something like this:

*'The essence of all beings is the earth, essence of the earth is water, essence of water is vegetation, essence of vegetation is man, essence of man is speech, essence of speech is the hymn of Rigveda, essence of Rigveda hymn is Saman (hymn-song of Samaveda), essence of Saman is Udgītha (up-beat song Om)'.*

# ANATOMICALLY MODERN HUMANS

'Anatomically modern human' refers only to the *'Homo sapiens'* species whereas 'human' refers to all the species of the genera *'Homo'*.

***Homo sapiens* species evolved in Africa about 200,000 years ago. There does not seem to be any evidence for different parallel evolutionary origins of the anatomically modern humans in India or anywhere else in the world.**

These anatomically modern humans were more ingenious and became expert savannah hunter-gatherers. Severe glacial period from 170,000 to 130,000 years ago nearly wiped out the game that these humans were hunting. Thus the anatomically modern humans faced near-extinction, and their population fell to about 10,000 or so.

Starting about 140,000 years ago, to supplement game as a source of food, they had turned to **beachcombing** – browsing for food on the seashore, and gathering and eating shellfish and other marine products from the seashore.

By about 130,000 years ago there were no other humans in Africa other than the anatomically modern humans (2). But, by that time, in Asia and Europe there were several human species other than modern humans.

There were no anatomically modern humans outside Africa. There were no humans of any kind in Australia and the Americas.

There was a warm interglacial period around 125,000 years ago, and soon after that around 120,000 years ago some of the modern humans travelled out of sub-Saharan Africa into North Africa and then on to what is called Levant. The Levant is a narrow corridor by the sea between the Mediterranean Sea to the north-west and deserts to the south-east. It is mainly the present day Syria and the surrounding regions. But this first migration from Africa was extinguished by an ice age glaciation that followed after their exodus (2).

Modern humans remained only in Africa until the next successful migration out of Africa. This is said to have happened about 85,000 years ago or so (2).

At this time, although there were no other human species in Africa, there were several human species inhabiting Europe and Asia. Some of them persisted until about 30,000 years ago.

Recent gene sequencing studies of Neanderthal and Denisovan genomes indicate that there was some breeding between the non-African modern humans and the Neanderthals, and between some non-African modern humans and Denisovans outside of Africa.

Non-African modern humans have 2 to 4% Neanderthal alleles in their genome, and some Melanesians have an additional 4 to 6% of Denisovan alleles in their genomes (Wikipedia.org). **The interbreeding between the Neanderthals and the anatomically modern humans, occurred in Europe and Asia, not in Africa.**

All non-African people including the people of India are the descendants of a group of modern humans who exited Africa about 85,000 years ago. In a sense, all the people of the world are part of one family.

**The anatomically modern humans had arrived in India by about 75,000 year ago.**

## ROUTE OF MIGRATION OUT OF AFRICA

The timing and route of migration out of Africa were determined by climate changes. There were only two potential routs out of Africa – a northern route and a southern route. Only one route would be open for migration at a particular point in time depending upon the glacial cycle of climate change. Northern route would be open during the warm inter-glacial periods whereas the southern route would be open during the cold periods of glaciation.

The continent of Africa is physically connected to Eurasia only through the Sinai Peninsula in the north. Below the Sinai Peninsula, Africa is separated from Arabia by the Red Sea. At the southern end of the Red Sea there is a narrow strait called 'Gate of Grief' or Gate of Tears' (Bab-el-Mandeb). It is about 15 miles (25 kilometers) wide.

**The northern route:** Most of the last two million years has been an ice epoch. But brief warming of the earth's surface known as interglacial optimum has occurred two times in the recent past. The most recent was about 8,000 years ago lasting about 2,000 to 3,000 years. The earlier interglacial came 125,000 years ago. During this relatively warm period Sahara desert was a grassland, and all kinds of game from the south spread throughout North Africa and then across into Levant. The

Levant is a narrow corridor by the sea between the Mediterranean Sea to the north-west and deserts to the south-east. It is mainly the present day Syria and the surrounding regions. The *northern route* out of Africa was through the Sinai Peninsula in the north to the Levant (2).

**Southern route:** Extreme cold weather brings glaciations of ice ages. During these glacial periods, large volumes of water are held in ice-sheets which may be as thick as a mile. The sea levels fall. When sea levels are very low, the Red Sea effectively becomes a salt lake with very little exchange from the Indian Ocean. There is less evaporation, there is less rain, and the desert belts expand over large territories of land closing the northern route for migration. The strait at the southern end of the Red Sea becomes a narrow water channel broken up by reefs and islands so that humans can easily go across this *southern route* (2).

It appears that pre-modern human species crossed out of Africa through the northern route about three times before. The last successful one being 250,000 years ago. Similarly, they have crossed out of Africa through the southern route three other times. The last one about 160,000 years ago.

**Evidence for the pre-modern humans in India has been well**

**established.** In the Narmada River valley in Central India, a skull of a large-brained archaic human, dated to over 150,000 years ago, has been found. India is much richer in the stone artifacts. Lower Paleolithic tools dating from 670,000 years down to 160,000 years ago, and the Middle Paleolithic tools of 160,000 years ago are abundant in India. The earliest evidence of deliberate patterning of stone that had some symbolic purpose – regular scratches, cross-hatching, and notching of pieces of stone or mineral pigment blocks – dating to 300,000 to 150,000 years ago have been found in the sandstone caves of India. (2).

Furthermore, recent findings of human artifacts in the Siwalk Hills north of New Delhi, India, dating back to at least 2.6 million years ago, suggests that humans may have left Africa half a million years earlier than previously thought (wikipedia.org).

During brief periods of warm and humid climates, the northern route out of Africa is amenable for migratory movements and habitation. Because of the brevity of warm periods, it can turn into a deadly trap for humans who migrated out of Africa. This is what seems to have happened to the unsuccessful first migration out of Africa by the anatomically modern humans 120,000 years ago. (2).

During the extreme cold weather of glaciation there was a severe decrease in sea level 85,000 years ago followed by a dramatic and brief improvement towards 'normal' about 83,000 years ago. And then there was an even more severe decrease to 340 feet below present sea level about 65,000 years ago. The great exodus from Africa of the anatomically modern humans took place about 85,000 years ago through the southern route (2).

## THE GREAT EXODUS

The first migration out of Africa by the anatomically modern humans about 120,000 years ago was unsuccessful. During brief periods of warm and humid climates, the northern route is amenable for migratory movements and habitation. Because of the brevity of warm periods, it can turn into a deadly trap. This is what seems to have happened to the unsuccessful first migration.

The first migrants out of Africa died out in the Levant as the dry glacial condition returned causing North Africa and Levant to revert to extreme desert (2). As stated before, Levant is a narrow corridor by the sea between the Mediterranean Sea to the north-west and deserts to the south-east. It is mainly the present day Syria and the surrounding regions.

During the extreme cold weather of glaciation that followed the above unsuccessful migration, there was a severe decrease in sea level about 85,000 years ago. Only the southern route was open for migration at that time. The great exodus from Africa of the anatomically modern humans took place about 85,000 years ago through the southern route. (2).

They travelled along the shores of the Indian Ocean, beachcombing - browsing for food on the seashore, and gathering and eating shellfish and other marine products from the seashore - and colonizing India and Southeast Asia along the way, and arriving in Indonesia and also in New Guinea by 75,000 years ago. Because the sea levels were low, it was a dry walk all the way to the tip of Java. The full beachcombing route from the Red Sea was along the coast of Indian Ocean to India, and then extending along the Indo-Pacific coast to China and Japan. (2).

During the next severe sea level depression about 65,000 years ago the anatomically modern humans went island hopping in Southeast Asia. They then traveled from Timor to the coast of Arnhem Land in northern Australia.

As the sea levels have risen, much of the evidences of the beachcombing trek have submerged. Available archeological evidence comes from Malay Peninsula, New Guinea and Australia.

Tools from the modern human culture embedded in Toba volcanic ash of 74,000 years ago have been found near Penang, Malaysia.

Occupation of a rock shelter on the coast of Arnhem Land in northern Australia by modern humans is dated to around 60,000 years ago. Several methods of dating of the earth-material surrounding the skeleton of an anatomically modern human found at Lake Mungo in southeast Australia have confirmed it to be about 62,000 years old. (2). There is no evidence of the presence of any human species in Australia prior to the arrival of the anatomically modern humans by then.

## THE GENETIC STUDIES

The genetic heritage of the modern humans is said to have been derived from a small group of about 10,000 Africans living in Africa about 190,000 years ago.

Genetic studies have confirmed that all modern humans evolved in Africa, that the first exodus out of Africa into Levant was unsuccessful, that there was only one successful main exodus of anatomically modern humans from Africa about 85,000 years ago, and that all non-African modern humans descended from this movement. (2).

Genetic studies have been done on the present day people all over the world. There is a magnificent body of published genetic marker information on the Indian subcontinent. (2).

Because the nomenclature of the genetic branches particularly of the Y-chromosomal ones was not uniform in different studies, a consensus Y nomenclature has recommended the use of letters A through R for the male genetic branches. Stephen Oppenheimer (reference 2) has introduced names for these genetic branches aided by context and association so that they can be remembered.

## MITOCHONDRIAL DNA STUDIES

The different combinations of mutations of mitochondrial DNA in the present day living women around the world have been determined, and have been used to reconstruct a female family tree that can be traced backwards to the first mothers about 200,000 years ago.

This group of first mothers in Africa having the root female genetic line have been called *'Mitochondrial Eve'*. The Mitochondrial Eve was not one sole individual ancestor. It is a shared ancestral genetic type.

From the original African mothers of all modern humans, there were about thirteen or so available diversity of maternal lines or clans in Africa at the time of the great exodus. It is said that even today there are fifteen surviving African maternal lines that are older than 80,000 years (2). **Among the non-Africans, there is no maternal line older than 83,000 years.**

It is possible that more than one line of African mother clan exited Africa. But after several thousand years of living isolated in southern Asia, only one line survived and the others failed to reproduce.

## Out-of-Africa Mother-line

The original mix of genetic variations 'drifted' to become one genetic out-of-Africa founder mother type. This is called the *'genetic drift'*. From time to time, some mothers' lines will die out because they have no surviving daughters to reproduce. (2).

**The out of Africa founding mother line is the L3 line.** The age of L3 line is about 83,000 years. This founding mother line L3 does not mean that there was only one mother with L3. It probably consisted of many mothers with that mitochondrial DNA marker.

There is no diversity in one line. Because the genetic drift is random, if two or more groups had exited Africa, especially at different time periods, they would not have drifted down to the same single L3 line. (2).

This Out of Africa L3 mother line mutated and branched many times to populate the rest of the world.

## M and N daughter lines

The out of Africa Asian mother line *L3* gave rise to two daughter line mutations: **M** and **N**. These two branches have been named by Oppenheimer (2) as *Manju* and *Nasreen* respectively. Both these mutations occurred around the same time. The Manju seems to have originated in India, where as Nasreen branch seems to have originated somewhere west of India (not in India). The most likely point of origin of Nasreen seems to be at the Arabian Gulf which was not a gulf at the time; it was a shallow lake fed by Tigris and Euphrates rivers (2).

As the genetic frequencies of these two lines including their subsequent daughter lines are traced from west to east, there is a gradual transition. In the area of the present day Yemen the ratio of Nasreen to Manju is 5 to 1; this ratio gradually decreases to 1 to 1 east of the Indus River in India; further east in Bengal region of India the ratio reverses to 1 to 5 where Manju dominates. To the north and east of India, the ratio evens out again. But on the east coast of India, there is nearly all Manju line. This pattern is consistent with near local extinction as a consequence of the Toba volcanic explosion 74,000 years ago, with recovery of only Manju line on the east coast of India. (2).

## **M-line in India**

**The Manju (M) line is found only in the Asians.** One exception is that the M1 line moved back across the Red Sea into Ethiopia. It was a more recent recolonization of East Africa from Asia (2). **Manju line is not found in Levant and Europe.**

The Manju line attains greatest diversity in India with a high proportion of root and primary branch types. The oldest of the daughter branches of Manju-line the *M2* line dates to 73,000 years ago. The M2 line is strongly represented in the Chenchu hunter-gatherer tribal populations of the present-day Andhra Pradesh region with their own unique M2 variants. (2).

### N's daughter line in India

Nasreen (N) itself did not originate in India. It originated west of India at the Arabian Gulf area. But Nasreen's line is represented in India by her daughter line *R* named *Rohani* by Oppenheimer (2).

**Nasreen is different from Manju in that the daughter lines of Nasreen are found in Non-Africans throughout the world.**

*Rohani (R)* line is very prolific with many daughter lines. Rohani's daughter branches that have originated in India are not shared by any other region. These branches have been dated to around 73,000 years ago. The Rohani expansion in India seems to have occurred during the recovery phase of the Toba disaster. A deeply branched diversity in the Rohani genetic line in India makes a case for Rohani's origin in India. (2).

## NON-RECOMBINANT Y-CHROMOSOMAL DNA STUDIES

Non-recombinant Y-chromosomal DNA studies give a picture similar to the one by the mitochondrial DNA studies. The different combinations of mutations of non-recombinant Y-chromosomal DNA can be traced backwards to the first fathers in Africa *(African Adam)*. From the original African fathers of all modern humans, there were at least as many available diversity of paternal lines in Africa at the time of the great exodus as Mitochondrial Eve had daughters.

**Of all the father lines present in Africa prior to the exodus, only one line succeeded in giving rise to all non-African male lines.** All non-African branch lines are derived from this *M168* line. This out of Africa father line gave rise to three primary mutational son lines *C, D/E (YAP),* and *F,* named as **Cain, Abel, and Seth** (biblical sons of Adam) respectively by Oppenheimer (2). **These three primary mutational son lines seem to have originated right out of Africa in Arabia.**

Because the behavior of men differs from that of women, men have more variation in the number of their offspring than women. A few dominating men father considerably more children than other men. Whereas women tend to have more even number of children among them. The effect is that more male lines become extinct than the female lines. Also, because of the behavior difference, male gene lines tend to show a more adventurous intercontinental spared than the female lines. (2).

*Cain (C)* line, in addition to populating India, traveled rapidly along the coast of the Indian Ocean to become the first male founder in Eastern Indonesia, Australia and New Guinea and also continued beachcombing along the Indo-Pacific coast to Japan and Korea.

*Abel (D/E or YAP)* line split into two right out of Africa. The western line populated parts of the Middle East and went back to Africa to populate the northern parts of Africa. The eastern branch, like the Cain branch, followed the beachcombing coast to Indonesia but did not enter or establish in Australia.

**Seth line *(F)* spread to every corner of the non-African world. The Seth-line is the dominant-line in India.**

## Seth-line (F-line) dominates in India

The Cain (C) male line is present throughout India at a rate of about 5%. The Abel line is in very small numbers in India. The Seth's lines (F-lines) account for about 95% of Indian male lines, and have deep splits in its branches in India. Cain line's low rates and minimal presence of Abel lines in India could be explained by the devastating effect on India of the Toba volcanic explosion, with near extinction of Abel and Cain lines, and subsequent predominant recovery of Seth branches. (2).

Descendants of the Seth's line are the most numerous in the world, let alone outside Africa. Seth line had five genetic son branch lines of which *K* line, named *Krishna* by Oppenheimer, was the most prolific one. Another of Seth's genetic son lines, the *J* line, named *Jahangir* by Oppenheimer is also found in India.

## The prolific Krishna-line (K) of Seth

*Krishna (K)* is one of the five genetic son branches of Seth. Krishna in turn had five genetic son lines. One genetic son line of Krishna is *P* line, named *Polo* by Oppenheimer. Polo had only two genetic son lines *Q* and *R*, named respectively as *Quetzalcoatl* and *Ruslan* by Oppenheimer. This gets to be confusing.

*Ruslan* is a large clan and its main line is *M173*. Polo's genetic son M173 Ruslan, and Ruslan's genetic son line *M17* arose in India, and spread out to Central Asia and then to Europe and East Asia. The ancestral-tree of M17 is as follows:

*Out of Africa father – Seth – Krishna – Polo – Ruslan – and then M17.*

Highest rates and greatest diversity of the M17 line are found in India including the present day Pakistan. M17 reaches a rate of 47% in Punjab with an overall rate in India of 27%. Furthermore, both high frequency and high diversity of M17 are found among tribal populations of South India including Chenchu and Yadhava tribal groups. This indicates that M17 is indigenous to these tribal groups in India. Origin of M17 in India is dated to be around 36,000 years ago. Since then, M17 found its way through Kashmir, Central Asia and Russia, and then into Europe. Its European age has been estimated to be 23,000 years. (2).

All this refutes any theory that M17 is the male marker of 'male Aryan invasion' of India. M17 went from India to Europe, and not the other way around.

## Beachcombing trail east of India

Beachcombing is browsing for food on the seashore, and gathering and eating shellfish and other marine products from the seashore.

Anatomically modern humans arrived in India, South East Asia, and also Papua New Guinea prior to the Toba super volcanic eruption which occurred about 74,000 years ago.

Continuing on the beachcombing trail, mitochondrial DNA analysis of aboriginal groups of the Malay Peninsula has revealed that three-quarters of Semang group have their own unique mitochondrial genetic Manju and Nasreen lines, and have no specific connection to any other Eurasian population. This indicates that after arriving long ago, they have remained isolated in the jungles of the Malay Peninsula. (2).

Of the male Y branch, the least changed or root type Cain is found in the Eastern Indonesian Islands of the Moluccas and Nusa Tenggara, which the first beachcombers had to island-hop to get to Australia. (2).

Australia has two main local ancestral Y types. Cain line is commonest at 60%, and the other is Seth's Indian genetic son Krishna-line at about 30%. Abel line is not found in

Australia. Since their arrival 65,000 years ago, the Native Australians have evolved isolated from others.

Further, the 30% rate of Krishna line persists throughout Southeast Asia and up the Pacific coast to Korea. These patterns suggest that the first beachcombing route not only went to New Guinea and Australia but continued up the Pacific coast to China, Japan and Korea.

## **East and Central Asia**

East and Central Asia was populated by three genetic colonizations.

The oldest settlers were the beachcombers who travelled up around the Indo-Pacific coast to Japan and Korea, leaving local colonies along the way.

From these local costal colonies, the second wave of migrants went up the great Asian rivers through gaps in the huge Himalayan Mountains. Southeast Tibet and Qinghai Plateau may have been the first parts of Central Asia to be inhabited this way around 60,000 years ago.

The third group was from northern India going through the mountain passes west of the Himalayas, to Central Asia, particularly to the Asian part of Russia. This settlement occurring during mild period around 43,000 years ago. In addition, the first group of beachcombers who had reached China might have gone up the Yellow River into Central Asia during the same mild period. (2).

## EUROPE

**Europe was inhabited by Neanderthals way before any anatomically modern humans arrived there.** The Neanderthals with their larger brain were as advanced, if not more advanced, as the modern humans at the time. As the migration of modern humans expanded into Europe, the Neanderthals gradually retreated to present day Italy, then to southern France, and finally to Spain and Portugal. They co-existed since 35,000 years ago for about 7,000 years. There is genetic evidence of inter-breeding to some extent. Then the Neanderthals died out around 28,000 years ago.

**There were two different waves of modern human migrations into Europe.**

**The first wave** consisted of a smaller group arriving around 46,000 years ago. They came from somewhere west of India. About 50,000 years ago, there was a period of warming lasting only a few thousand years, an interstadial as it is called. It has been detected by a carbon-rich layer in the undersea delta of the Indus River. Climate improvement opened up a narrow green corridor west of the Zagros Mountains in present day Iran, allowing migration from the west of India to the Mediterranean Near East.

Low rates of the Nasreen (N mitochondrial DNA line) root type and a great variety of the Nasreen's genetic daughter line Rohani (R) are found only in South Asia. Most Rohani types in India are found nowhere else. The great diversity of Rohani type in India gives an estimated date of its expansion to be 55,000 years ago.

Rohani's daughter line ***U***, named *Europa* by Oppenheimer, is found in the Mediterranean Near East. There were seven U line daughters. The fifth daughter branch ***U5*** colonized Europe mainly along the Mediterranean coast. *U6* about the same age as U5 is not found in Europe. U6 moved west round the southern shore of the Mediterranean Sea into North Africa; U6 is a unique identifier of Berbers of Libya. (2).

Y-chromosomal DNA line Seth (F line) is even more specific as to the trek to Europe. One of Seth's genetic sons ***J***, named *Jahangir* by Oppenheimer, has a South Asian origin. Jahangir is found at about 59% frequency in the southernmost part of the Zagros Mountains region. Mediterranean distribution of Jahangir mirrors the spread of U5 and U6 as above.

**The second wave** of invasion of Europe was a larger one, arriving there around 33,500 years ago and thereafter. Another daughter line of Rohani is the *HV* line.

The roots of HV line are found in north-west India, and dated to be around 40,000 years ago. The two genetic daughter lines **H** and **V** are found throughout Europe today. The H descendants are half of all western and northern European maternal lines, Slav, Finn and Germanic in particular. There is a considerably younger and a smaller back-migration from Europe to the Mediterranean Near East. (2).

Again the Y-chromosomal DNA is more specific with a good trail. The three male genetic lines of the second and larger invasion of Europe are all descendants of the Krishna (K) line.

*Ruslan (**R** line)* arising in India from the Polo (P) line goes directly north through mountain passes to Central Asia where he splits east and west to East Asia and Europe. Ruslan is the progenitor of half of all Europe's men. Ruslan's genetic son line **M17** comes to Europe later, and achieves the highest frequency of 60% in Hungarians with lower frequencies in all parts of western and southern Europe and the Mediterranean Near East. The third Krishna line is called **TAT**. It originates in Central Asia from the line coming from Kashmir in India, and is mostly confined to the eastern fringe of Europe among Baltic Finns and Russians.

## **The Last Glacial Maximum**

The Last Glacial Maximum, as it is called, is the highest of the big freezes. It was the last period in the Earth's climate history during the last glacial period when ice sheets were at their greatest extension. Growth of ice sheets reached their maximum positions 24,500 BCE. Deglaciation commenced in the Northern Hemisphere gradually between 18,000 BCE and 17,000 BCE (wikipedia.org).

Icecaps grew and occupied larger territories and some of them were three miles thick. The sea level decreased to an astonishing 400 feet below present level. The world's deserts expanded enormously. Huge areas of land became totally uninhabitable. Living and movement of human populations in the northern areas were disrupted.

The ice-sheets were not evenly distributed. Central and northwestern regions of Europe were covered in ice as were the mountainous regions. But Eastern Europe and most of North and Central Asia remained ice-free.

North America was severely affected. Two massive ice sheets covered Canada, Great Lakes and the northeastern United States. But Alaska on the other hand was not covered with ice. It was connected to Siberia by dry land called **Beringia**. From 25,000 to 22,000 years ago there was a narrow path between the two massive ice sheets down to the rest of the America. But between 22,000 and 15,000 years ago the two North American icecaps closed off this narrow corridor to the lower parts of the Americas.

Low sea level also resulted in India joining up with Sri Lanka, Japan becoming connected to Asian mainland, Australia and New Guinea joining to form the continent of Sahul, and Indo-China, Malaysia and Islands of Indonesia merging with dry land to form a vast landmass called Sundaland.

## The America

Prior to the onset of *'The Last Glacial Maximum'* there was no human being present in the Americas except in Beringia (see below).

Prior to the onset of the Last Glacial Maximum, because of worsening conditions in Asia, anatomically modern humans had moved over from Asia on to the dry land Beringia. From 25,000 to 11,000 years ago Bering Strait was a land bridge with grassy tundra supporting herbivorous animals. But from 22,000 to 15,000 years ago Beringia and Western Alaska were cut off from both continents – Siberia in Asia was an arctic desert, and the two North American icecaps closed off the corridor south to the lower parts of the Americas.

Four American founder mitochondrial DNA lines have been identified and have been traced back to respective branches *A, B, C* and *D* in Asia, all descending from the original Manju (M) and Nasreen (N) lines. Subsequent reanalysis has added another founder clan *X* (from N line), to make a total of five American founder mother lines. These founder lines came to Beringia before the Last Glacial Maximum, and spread throughout the Americas before the corridor to the south closed off.

Estimated average age of A through D lines is 23,000 years in North America, 16,000 years in Central America and 21,000 years in South America. When Beringia was cut off from both the continents, it became a refuge holding the remnants of the original founder lines that dwindled down to a derived type A2 and nothing else. Where as in the rest of the Americas, all founding groups (A through D, and X) were widely distributed and were diverse. Americas are huge and there are marked differences in the relative frequencies of the five mitochondrial founder lines among the Native American People.

The male Y-chromosomal studies reveal that one line dominates all the Americas. Over 90% of all modern Native American male lines derive from the Polo (P) line, one of the genetic son lines of Krishna (K line).

Although the Polo line accounts for 50% of the Europeans, most of the European subtypes are not the same as those of the Americans. Of the two genetic son lines of Polo, Q (Quetzalcoatl) and R (Ruslan), the Q line dominates and is unique to the Native Americans. Q also has been dated to have come from Asia to America 22,000 years ago. In addition to the Polo line, another Krishna line TAT line is found rarely among the Americans. In addition to all the above original Seth male line, another Y chromosomal line is derived from Cain beachcombing line.

All the above genetic findings suggest that the founder lines made multiple parallel entries from Northeastern Asia and the East coast of Asia, into the Americas just prior to the onset of Last Glacial Maximum.

## ONE FAMILY

All the peoples of the world belong to one big family that originated in Africa. Adaptation, mutation and genetic drift have made us what we are today. There is no superiority gene in any one or more groups of people among us.

In a different context this is what Ishavasya Upanishad (reference 4) says in its sixth verse:

*'One who perceives all beings as not distinct from one's own Self, and one's own Self as the Self of all beings, that one, by virtue of that perception, does not hate anyone.'*

Similarly Bhagavd-Gita (reference 5) verse 29 in chapter six says something like this:

*'A realized individual, the mind harmonized by yoga, sees one's own Self in all beings, sees all beings in one's own Self, and sees the same in all, and makes no distinction whatsoever'.*

## THE THEORY OF ARYAN INVASION OF INDIA IS A FALLACY

The theory of Aryan invasion of India had been put forward in the nineteenth century of Common Era (CE/AD) to explain the ancient history of India. According to this theory, India was invaded and conquered around 1,500 Before Common Era (BCE/BC) by nomadic light-skinned Indo-European tribes from central Asia (6). That meant that there was no trace of Aryan history or the Sanskrit language in India prior to this invasion, and that Religion, philosophy, literature, and everything else were due to the activities of these Aryans subsequent to their arrival in India after 1,500 BCE.

The theory argued that the Vedic Aryans entered India from the northwest through the mountain passes of Afghanistan; they were barbaric semi-nomadic tribes who came in search of new grazing land for their cattle; they came down on horseback and chariots, armed with swords, bows and arrows, and other weapons, and were ruthless in conquering and subduing the native population. In that process, they supposedly destroyed the existing political, economic and religious order (7).

The false theory of Aryan invasion of India came about in the 19th century when the British were ruling India. In India the British scholars discovered the Vedas composed in the beautiful and perfect language of Sanskrit. They could not believe that the ancient people of India could come up with the Vedas and Sanskrit. They noticed that there were some similarities between Sanskrit and some of the European languages. Instead of considering the possibility that the homeland of these languages could be India itself, and thus looking for the evidences, the European scholars invented this theory, stating that the ancient people of India were uncivilized and therefore could not have come up with the language of Sanskrit and the Vedas.

The so called Pre-Aryan inhabitants of India were labelled as 'Dravidians', who, they claimed, had been driven down to the southern parts of India by the Aryans, mainly to the present day Tamilnadu State (previously called Madras State). They had implicated Tamil as the main language of the Dravidians, and had included Kannada and Telugu as other Dravidian languages.

According to the false Aryan Invasion Theory, the uncivilized dark-skinned Dravidians with their Dravidian languages were the ancient inhabitants of India.

The British who were ruling India had adamantly asserted that this false theory was factual, and taught it in schools as such.

**The basic fallacy of the theory was the assumption that the dark-skinned ancient people of India could not have, on their own, come up with such a perfected Sanskrit language and the Vedas.**

### The Language Issue

Why is it then that the Europeans did not compare the language of Sanskrit to the so called Dravidian languages, and consider the possibility that India was the homeland of Sanskrit and the Vedas?

It is hard to answer this question, but the comparison of the languages is as follows.

Kannada language had been labelled as one of the Dravidian languages, and it was implied that it was in use in India more than one thousand years prior to the so called Aryan invasion. When you compare Kannada and Sanskrit, you would see the following:

- Kannada and Sanskrit languages have the same type of the alphabet with the same type of pronunciation. Kannada has two more vowels than Sanskrit.

- There is more than 50% concordance in the words and phrases of the two languages and their meanings.

Basically, Sanskrit and Kannada are very similar languages. Further, there is not much difference between Kannada and Telugu, and Tamil is somewhat similar. Some of the European languages had measly a few words that were similar to Sanskrit whereas the languages themselves of the ancient people of India, not just a few words, were similar to that of Sanskrit. Why is it then that the Europeans did not consider the possibility that India was the homeland of Sanskrit and the Vedas?

One explanation could be that this language similarity was brought up, but it was simply dismissed.

The point is not that Sanskrit is derived from Kannada, it is that Sanskrit was the original language, and all languages of India, including Kannada and the other so called Dravidian languages of southern India are derived from the original Sanskrit language of ancient India. (Also see 'Sanskrit Script' article in this book.)

### Civilization Issue

This false theory was not founded on any archeological evidence.

The Aryan invasion theory had been put forward before the archeological discoveries of the large urban ruins of the Indus valley culture at Harappa and Mohenjo-

Daro, which showed a far advanced civilization in ancient India dating around 3,100 BCE. (See 'Archaeological Findings of the Vedic Civilization' article in this book.)

It was astonishing to everyone that the archeological findings revealed a very advanced civilization in ancient India during that time. It was astonishing mainly because the European scholars had falsely convinced the whole world that, prior to the so called Aryan Invasion of India between 1,500 BCE and 1,200 BCE, there was no recognizable civilization in India, and that the people inhabiting ancient India were almost barbarians leading a life of nomads.

Advanced civilization is required in order to come up with any perfected language and a sophisticated literature. India was the home to such an advanced civilization. There was no recognizable civilization in west-central Asia. Then, how is it possible for the uncivilized people of central Asia to possess such Sanskrit and Vedas?

After the discovery, instead of rectifying the false theory, there was even more speculation that the native people who had been labeled as 'Dravidians' might not have been the natives, but some other people who had come to India at some prior time and had established such an advanced civilization (6, 7). This again was based on the assumption that the ancient people of India could not have possibly established such an advanced civilization. Of course, this speculation has been proven wrong (8).

If the basic assumption for the theory is wrong, then the theory that is based on that assumption is also wrong.

### Ancient Literature Issue

The false Aryan invasion of India theory was not based on any historical records.

**There is no literary or historical record of any such event until this false theory of the 19th century CE. All the world literature up until this false theory does not mention any such invasion.**

Some scholars have claimed that the expedition of Aryans into India is mentioned several times in Rigveda. This is not true.

**It must be pointed out to the readers that nowhere in Rigveda there is anything about the foreigners invading India.**

The claims which state that the Aryan invasion is mentioned in Rigveda, use 'Dasyu', 'Paṇi', and other terms contemptuously when referring to the ancient people of India who had been falsely labelled as the 'Dravidians'.

Dasyus, Paṇis, and others were the same group of people as the 'Āryas', but they had become more materialistic and had fallen out of the spiritual culture of the seers. They were those among the same people, who did not follow the spiritual rules. Many of those non-followers were reinstated as Āryas once they purified themselves and started following the spiritual Vedic rules. Some who did not were driven away by the kings. The kings follow the wisdom of their ruling priests, and protect the sacrifice and guard the spiritual life of the Āryas.

Rigveda verse I.51.8 is as follows (1, 9): *Discern between the Āryas and them who are Dasyus; restraining those who perform no religious rites, compel them to submit to the performance of sacrifice: (Indra) be you who are powerful, the encourager of the sacrifice. I am desirous of celebrating all your deeds in ceremonies that give you satisfaction.*

Rigveda verse VIII.64.2 is as follows (1, 9): *Crush with your foot the Paṇis who offer no oblations; (Indra) you are mighty, there is none so ever like unto you.*

It is clear from the above verses of Rigveda that the Aryas, Dasyus, and Panis were the same group of people with different spiritual inclination. They were not the so called Aryans and Dravidians.

Neither the so-called conquering people, nor the so-called conquered people of India have any memory or record of such an immense event if it ever happened. To date there is no culture in ancient India that can be identified as that of the 'invading Aryans'. The so-called 'Vedic Aryans' were indigenous to India. The term 'Aryan' is an anglicized word with an 'n' at the end of the Sanskrit word 'arya' meaning 'noble' or 'cultured'. The ancients, who transmitted the sacred heritage of the Vedas, described themselves as the 'Aryas' (7). They could not have been the invading barbarians. (See 'Arya' article that comes next in this book.)

**Invasion route, horse and chariot issues**

The invasion theory had argued that the Aryans entered India from the northwest through the mountain passes of Afghanistan, and that they came down on horseback and chariots.

The northwest mountain passes to ancient India were treacherous and were not easy to pass. The invaders could not have been able to pass using the chariots. Trekking and may be horseback traveling was possible. The horses of central Asia are different from the horses of India and Arabia. The central Asian horses have eighteen pairs of ribs with a total of 36 ribs, but the horses in India and the Arabian horses have seventeen pairs of ribs with a total of 34 ribs. If the invaders had come with their horses, then those horses should have had 36 ribs. Further, if invaders had brought their Rigveda with them, then that Rigveda should have said that the horses have 36 ribs. That is not the case. Rigveda says that the horse has 34 ribs.

Rigveda sukta I.162 describes the horse sacrifice which the kings have it performed by employing various priests and others. Verse 18 in that sukta is as follows (9):

*The axe penetrates the thirty-four ribs of the swift horse: the beloved gods cut up with skill so that the limbs may be unperforated, and recapitulating joint by joint.*

As can be seen from the above Rigveda verse, the horses had 34 ribs. The Rigveda and the horses did not come from central Asia; they were indigenous to ancient India.

Horse genetics also has confirmed that the horses did not come from central Asia. They were indigenous to India.

### Rigveda and the Sarasvati River

The Rigveda speaks of, and praises the mighty river **Sarasvati**, the largest of the seven rivers forming the life support of the Vedic civilization in ancient India. Three sūktas in Rigveda are dedicated to Sarasvati. Sukta VI.61 has 14 verses, and suktas VII.95 and

VII.96 have six verses each. Sarasvati River is glorified in these suktas:

*This Sarasvati flows rapidly with all sustaining waters, sweeping in its might all other waters. Sarasvati, chief and pure of rivers, flowing from the mountains to the ocean, and distributing riches among the many existing beings. The most mighty river with those your waves, Sarasvati, the distributor of water, be our protector.*

The satellite imagery has revealed that the Thar Desert in India, also called the Great Indian Desert, was once traversed by this great river, flowing from the Tibetan Himalayas to the Arabian Sea (7). Around 1,900 BCE, over a comparatively short period of time, major tectonic shifts occurred which drastically altered the flow of rivers and turned the Sarasvati region into inhospitable desert. Prior to the final demise, the Sarasvati River had shifted its course at least four times, gradually turning the region inhospitable. Eastward migration of the Vedic people occurred over several hundred years prior to the catastrophe of 1,900 BCE. Shatapatha Brahmana of the Shukla Yajurveda vividly describes the conquest of the swampy area east of the Ganges River (7).

Since the archaeological discovery of Harappa and Mohenjo-Daro, hundreds of other sites have been described. Most of the sites are situated in the desert plains in India formerly watered by several rivers including the Sarasvati River which was larger than the Indus River. (See 'Archaeological Findings of the Vedic Civilization' article in this book.)

All this indicates that the Vedic civilization existed in ancient India way before 1,900 BCE, and that Sanskrit and the Vedas were indigenous to India.

### Astronomical references in Rigveda

Rigveda has many astronomical references in it. Author David Frawley in his book (reference 10) on pages 165 through 199 explains the astronomical references in detail. According to his explanation, the astronomical references in Rigveda go as far back as 6,000 BCE, and may even be before that time. On the basis of his analysis, he gives the dates for the Vedic texts as follows:

Proto-Rigveda period: Before 6,000 BCE

Early Rigveda period: 6,000 BCE through 4,000 BCE

Late Rigveda period (also four Veda period): 4,000 BCE through 2,000 BCE.

This information corresponds with the archaeologic findings (see 'Archaeological Findings of the Vedic Civilization' article in this book).

## The Genetics

**Genetics, both in regard to human and animal (particularly cattle and horses) populations, is offering new evidence. Human populations in India show persistence of the same population groups with no evidence of an intrusion of populations that could alter the genetics of humans in India at the time of the so-called invasion** (2, 6).

## New model of ancient India

The new model of ancient India is that of an indigenous development of civilization in ancient India from about 10,000 BCE to the present day. The people of this tradition are the same basic ethnic groups as in India today, with their same basic types of languages. It makes the Vedic India perhaps the oldest, longest and most central of the world's cultures (6)

The Rigveda period had been well established during the period prior to 3,100 BCE. The beginning of this Rigveda period is generally considered by the Indian scholars to be around 10,000 BCE (13).

The so labeled 'Dravidians' were the original Arya people of India. There was no Aryan-Dravidian division; everyone belonged to the same Ārya people.

From the beginning of the recognizable civilization in India, the ancient people of India were the Āryas - not Aryans with an 'n' at the end.

The people of south India are Āryas; they are not distinguishable separately as Aryans or Dravidians (page 127 of reference 11); they have been falsely labeled as Dravidians. The Āryas of the south, who have been labeled as 'Dravidians', have been the best preservers of the Vedic culture.

The best Vedic Sanskrit, the rituals and traditions are found only in the South of India (page 44 of reference 6). The Āryas of the south have better preserved the Vedas than the north.

The 'Theory of Aryan Invasion of India' is erroneous, and there is no evidence whatsoever of such an invasion.

# ĀRYA

The word 'Ārya' is a Sanskrit word. It is not the same as the anglicized word 'Aryan' which has an 'n' at the end. The word 'Ārya' does not have an 'n' at the end.

*'Vishvadevas (the Universal Gods) generated prayer, the cow, the horse, the earth, the waters and the hills; these very bounteous Gods made the Sun mount to the heaven, and spread the righteous laws of Ārya over the land'.* Says Rigveda X.65.11 (reference 1).

The Sanskrit word Ārya means 'noble' or 'pure', and refers to a person with high mind and good spiritual values (10). Āryas were the original Vedic people of ancient India. To them the ancient India was known as Āryavarta, the abode of the Ārya.

*'I (Indra) have bestowed the earth upon the Ārya, and rain upon the man who brings oblation'.* Says Rigveda IV.26.2 (reference 1).

Homeland of the ancient Vedic people was mainly the Sarasvati River region. The Sarasvati River which was to the east of the Indus River, has gone dry. The ancients resided there for a long time before the hymns of the Rigveda were finalized (page 76 of reference 10). Subsequently the main homeland included the Ganga (Ganges),

Yamuna and the Sarasvati River regions. In addition, the greater Vedic land included the surrounding vast areas – the northern region consisting of what is now the Punjab and the mountains of Kashmir, the western region of Gandhara extending into Afghanistan, the southern region by the Arabian Sea, and the eastern region marked by the Bay of Bengal (page 95 of reference 10).

In the ancient times, the livelihood of the Āryas depended mainly on raising cattle (12). They constantly herded their cattle from one grazing ground to another. In order to protect the cattle during harsh weather, the cattle were kept in secure shelters. A shelter for cattle is called *gotra* in Sanskrit. As there were a relatively small number of these gotras, many families shared the same gotra in their area. To resolve any disputes among them, they appointed a supervisor called a *Gotrapati.* The overseers were selected on the basis of their great moral and spiritual virtues. Some of them attained the highest spiritually illumined status and were recognized as the great Rishis (seers/sages). The groups of Ārya families used the Gotrapati name to identify their 'Gotra', and forbid marriage among the members of the same Gotra to prevent any inbreeding (12). Nowadays this strict rule is sometimes not followed. Agriculture was gradually developed, and along with the animal husbandry, it became the main means of livelihood.

**The term Ārya did not refer to any particular race, religion or language**, but referred to a moral quality or mental disposition, that of nobility, uniting the like-minded into a kinship (7). Ārya culture was based upon the rule of the seers of the Rigveda. In this regard those who followed the spiritual culture of the seers were the Āryas. Those among the same people, who did not follow the spiritual rules, were considered as the fallen Aryas ('fallen-Aryas' is an explanatory term used here in this book). Dasyus, Paṇis, and others (the fallen-Āryas) were the same group of people as the 'Āryas', but they had become more materialistic and had fallen out of the spiritual culture of the seers. They were those among the same people, who did not follow the spiritual rules. Many of these fallen-Āryas were reinstated as Āryas once they purified themselves and started following the spiritual Vedic rules. Some who did not were kind of driven away.

Āryas called their spiritual system *'Ārya Dharma'* which means religious duties of the Āryas. Although the Sanskrit word Dharma has other meanings, here it means religion or religious duties (12).

Āryas also called their religion *'Mānava Dharma'* which means 'Religion of Man'; it meant that it belonged to the whole of mankind (12). Another term they used was *'Sanatana Dharma'* which means 'The Eternal Religion'; it implied that it was based on eternal truths (12). In relatively recent times, Buddha of Buddhism also used the term 'Ārya Dharma' for his teachings of the laws of Āryas (10).

Social life was permeated by spiritual consciousness. Truth and righteousness were extolled. Civilization became well developed, and fine arts were encouraged (13). As kings and priests became powerful, the system of sacrifices evolved into higher degree of perfection (13).

As indicated above the Ārya homeland was mainly to the east of the Indus River. The neighboring Persians, west of ancient India, apparently pronounced the word Sindhu as Hindu, and called the Āryas as the Hindus. Hence Ārya Dharma came to be known as Hinduism (12).

The Ārya people of India, including those of south India whose culture was also the Vedic culture, place themselves in the lineage of the Vedic seers. The descendants of their families are also considered as descendants of these seers, and they identify themselves as such (10).

The people of south India are Āryas; they are not distinguishable separately as

Aryans or Dravidians (page 127 of reference 11); they have been labeled as Dravidians. The Āryas of the south have been the best preservers of the Vedic culture. The best Vedic Sanskrit, the rituals and traditions are found only in the South of India (page 44 of reference 6). The Aryas of the south trace their culture back to the great Rigveda Rishi (sage) Agastya whose representation is found in all the temples of south India (10). The Āryas of the south have better preserved the Vedas than the north.

The Rigveda is mostly in use in western India including Maharashtra and Karnataka. Karnataka people are the Rigveda people. In Andhra Pradesh region, 98% of the people belong to Yajurveda and only 2% to Rigveda; in Tamil Nadu which included Kerala until about a thousand years ago, Samavedis predominated in the past, but in later times only 15% are Samavedis, about 5% are Rigvedis, and Yajurvedis predominate at about 80% (page128 of reference 11).

# ARCHAEOLOGICAL FINDINGS OF THE VEDIC CIVILIZATION

The most extraordinary finding of Indian archaeology is that there is no noticeable break in the series of cultural developments from 8,000 BCE to modern India (7). In the Indian Subcontinent, a continuous sequence of dwelling-sites from 7,000 BCE has been established.

## **The Discovery**

It was the building of India's railway system in the nineteenth century of the Common Era (CE) that revealed the secrets of the Vedic Civilization (14). British were ruling India then.

Two British engineer-brothers, in the year 1856, were having difficulty laying tracks for the East India Railway on the sandy soil in the Indus River valley area, and were looking for some hard material to be used for the railroad bed. One of the brothers heard about a nearby ancient ruined city called Brahminabad, and he went there. The Brahminabad city had been built using hard well-burnt bricks. He took the bricks from there and used them to strengthen the railroad bed. Brahminabad was later named as Mohenjo-Daro. Similarly, north of there, the other brother found another city called Harappa, and plundered the prehistoric city of

Harappa for ballast. They used these ancient bricks to lay down about 93 miles of railroad tracks. Some invaluable evidence was destroyed in that plundering.

General Sir Alexander Cunningham, when he was the Director General of the Indian Archaeological Survey, excavated the area in the year 1872. He published the discovery in 1875, but it went unnoticed.

In the year 1920, Sir John Marshall, the then Director General of Archaeology in India, sent an Indian archaeologist Daya Ram Sahni to start excavating the mounds of Harappa; and in 1922 another Indian archaeologist R. D. Banerji started to excavate at the Mohenjo-Daro site. In 1931, Sir John Marshall published a detailed account of the archaeological findings in a book called 'Mohenjo-Daro and Indus Civilization'. In that book, he proposed that the Harappa Age matured during the period from 3,100 BCE to 2,750 BCE (8, 14).

In the year 1947, at the time of independence from the British, India was partitioned into India and Pakistan. The above two sites are in the present day Pakistan. Since then hundreds of other sites have been discovered in India proper.

Then in the year 1974, archaeologists made another startling and far-reaching discovery – the discovery of the town of Mehrgarh in Baluchistan of the present day

Pakistan (7). The excavations at the site have yielded an early date of around 7,000 BCE. There is no noticeable break in the series of cultural developments from Mehrgarh to Harappa to modern India.

## **Mehrgarh**

The Mehrgarh site covers an area of over 500 acres, and it has a number of successive settlements dated between 7,000 BCE to 2,600 BCE. It is one of the earliest sites with evidence of farming wheat and barley, and herding cattle, sheep and goats.

The oldest of the settlements was a farming village dated between 7,000 BCE and 5,500 BCE. The early Mehrgarh residents lived in rectangular mud-brick houses, stored grain in granaries, fashioned tools with local copper ore, and lined their large basket containers with bitumen (Wikipedia.org).

At the oldest site, three primitively fashioned human figurines made out of un-fired clay have been found (7).

It is astonishing to note that evidence for the drilling of teeth in living persons was found in Mehrgarh. Eleven drilled molar crowns from nine adults have been discovered in a Neolithic graveyard dating from 7,500 to 9,000 years ago. It is the oldest and the first evidence in human history for drilling the teeth in living persons (Wikipedia.org).

The Mehrgarh site showed that during the periods from 5,500 BCE to 3,500 BCE, pottery was in use, beads decorated with opaque colored glazes were produced, terracotta figurines became more detailed, and button-seals were produced from terracotta and bone material; the seals had geometric designs. The figurines are thought to be some religious objects; some of them may represent mother goddess.

Mehrgarh is considered as a precursor to the Indus-Sarasvati civilization; the archaeological findings show a continuous series of cultural developments from Mehrgarh to Harappa and then to modern India.

### **The Harappan World**

Since the archaeological discovery of Harappa and Mohenjo-Daro, hundreds of other sites have been described. In addition to large urban centers, the landscape of ancient India was dotted with numerous villages and towns.

The Harappan World covers an area around 300,000 square miles, stretching from the Himalayas in the north to the Godavari River in modern Karnataka in the south of India, and from the Indus River in the west to the plains of Ganges and Yamuna Rivers in the east. Most of the sites are situated in the desert plains in India formerly watered by several rivers including the Sarasvati River which was larger than the Indus River. [Explanation of the now extinct Sarasvati River is given in the article 'Timing of the Vedic Civilization.] The Harappan Vedic culture area by far exceeds in size the combined area occupied by the Sumerian and the Egyptian Civilizations (6, 7).

## **The Findings**

Detailed explanation of the archaeological findings is beyond the scope of this article and the book. Brief descriptions are given here (7, 8, and 14).

The layout of the settlements, which is said to be well planned, is regular with streets crossing one another at right angles. The larger cities and towns have been divided into districts, and a high rectangular fortress like structure with bath houses and a granary commands the view of the rest of the city to the east.

The houses, some are two or more stories high, are built of standardized baked bricks. Each house has several rooms around a square courtyard. The houses have bathrooms which are connected by drains to the brick-lined sewers underneath the main street. The houses open on to the small side-streets, not to the main streets. All this was about 5,000 years ago.

Numerous sacrificial fire-altars, mostly

of rectangular or square shape and some of round or ovoid shape constructed with burnt-bricks are found all over ancient India. Some of the sacrificial fire-altars contained ashes of charcoal and the offerings of beads and gold and such.

There is a great deal of evidence to show that trade was various and wide-ranging. City of Lothal, at the head of the Gulf of Cambay in India, has the largest brick structure known to have been built then. The so-called Warf of Lothal measures 230 yards by 40 yards. The Lothal city served as a seaport. Furthermore, remarkable system of weights and measures has been found.

Striking pieces of art have been found. Clay figurines probably representing the mother goddess, bust of a bearded man probably representing a priest, superb artistic sculpture of male torso, 'dancing-girl' figurine, a bronze artifact which has been called as 'Vasishṭha head', and many other artifacts have been found. Vasishṭha is the great seer of Rigveda. He is the most famous of the Vedic sages, and has the most hymns in Rigveda.

The excavations in India have been particularly rewarding in the number of recovered seals. Thousands have been found, mostly of square or rectangular shape. This is in contrast to the mostly round seals of

Mehrgarh. Many seals carry glyphs of neatly designed script dated to as far back as 3,300 BCE. (See 'Sanskrit Script' article in this book.) Many other seals depict animals including the bull-unicorn and the humped bull, and some show humans.

## **Shiva**

One type of remarkable soapstone seals of particular interest, many experts agree, is an early representation of 'Shiva' as 'Pashupati' which means 'Lord of the Beasts'. The Shiva figure is seated cross-legged straight on a throne-like pedestal, with outstretched arms resting on the knees in the so-called lotus-position of the Yoga. On the head there is an elaborate head-gear which has two symmetrical horns. The face is somewhat mask-like, there might be an extension of the head-gear on to the face. The chest and arms are decorated with ornaments or adorned with sacred ash (vibhuti). There is a representation of a decorated belt on the waist. At the top portion of the seal above the Shiva figure, there are six symbols or glyphs. On either side of the figure, there is an elephant facing away from, and a rhinoceros, a buffalo and a tiger facing toward the figure. At the bottom portion of the seal there are two antelopes.

It is notable that Sir John Marshall, in his book, states: 'None perhaps is more remarkable than this discovery that Shaivism has a history going back to the Chalcolithic Age (4,300 BCE to 3,300 BCE), or perhaps even further still, and that it thus takes its place as the most ancient living faith in the world' (on page 36 of reference 8).

## TIMING OF THE VEDIC CIVILIZATION

The Vedas are the most sacred scriptures of the people of India, particularly for the Hindus. It is said that the Vedas are without a beginning because they contain the ever present divine revelations. Rigveda is the most ancient of all compositions of the revelations. It was fashioned along with the ancient Sanskrit which was purely an oral literature in the past. Although it is extremely difficult to place the beginning of this Rigveda period, it is generally considered by the Indian scholars to be around 10,000 Before Common Era (BCE) (reference 13).

It is to be emphasized that the Civilization of India is the Vedic Civilization.

India has emerged as the oldest continuous civilization on earth. New biological evidence suggests that the Indian population has lived in the peninsula for at least the past 75,000 years.

In addition to the older archeological finds in Harappa and Mohenjo-Daro, and in Mehrgarh (all in present day Pakistan), significant new sites relating to Indian antiquity have been discovered (7).

Sites discovered along the Indus River, including the Harappa and Mohenjo-Daro sites, have been, in the past, referred collectively as pertaining to the 'Indus

Civilization'. However, many more archeological sites than those have been discovered in the area where the ancient mighty Sarasvati River was (see below). It may be more appropriate to call the civilization as 'Indus-Sarasvati Civilization'.

The earliest Indic art dated to be as far back as 40,000 BCE is preserved on rocks, and dates from the Paleolithic to the Mesolithic and Neolithic periods. The rock sites are found distributed all over India. A continuity of the central theme between the rock art as above and the art of the Indus-Sarasvati civilization of 8,000 BCE to 1,900 BCE has been found. According to the archeological record, there is an unbroken tradition going back to 8,000 BCE. Rigveda, a compilation of very ancient material, has astronomical references recalling events in the third to the fifth millennia BCE and earlier, indicating that the Rigveda period had been well established during that period prior to 3,100 BCE (7).

The ancient Indus-Sarasvati civilization reached its maturity by 2,700 BCE. It was the golden age of the Vedas when the Vedic religious practice was in vogue. The practice was based on all the Vedas. The composition of the main parts of the four Vedas had been completed by then with some of the appendages added at a later date.

The Rigveda speaks of, and praises the mighty river **Sarasvati**, the largest of the seven rivers forming the life support of the Vedic civilization in ancient India.

The satellite imagery has revealed that the Thar Desert in India, also called the Great Indian Desert, was once traversed by this great river, flowing from the Tibetan Himalayas to the Arabian Sea (7). Originally the Sarasvati flowed through Rajasthan and poured itself into the Gulf of Kuch near Kathilawar Peninsula. One of the main tributaries was the Yamuna River which now flows into Ganga (Ganges) River. Sutledge River was also a tributary of Sarasvati; it now flows into the Indus River.

Around 1,900 BCE, over a comparatively short period of time, major tectonic shifts occurred which drastically altered the flow of rivers and turned the Sarasvati region into inhospitable desert – the present day Thar Desert in India. Prior to the final demise, the Sarasvati River had shifted its course at least four times, gradually turning the region inhospitable.

Shatapatha (Hundred Paths) Brahmana of the Shukla (white) Yajurveda, the biggest of all the Brahmanas, vividly describes the conquest of the swampy area east of the Ganges River, and does not mention the drying up of the Sarasvati River. This indicates that the eastward migration of the Vedic people occurred over several hundred years prior to the catastrophe of 1,900 BCE and that the Shatapatha Brahmana was composed during that time period (7).

Ganga (Ganges) River valley had been inhabited at least since 5,000 BCE. It was a thickly forested swampy area with heavy monsoon rains. Forest had to be cleared to make room for the new settlements. The center of vitality shifted from west to east, from the Sarasvati to the Ganga (Ganges). Remembrance of the period of forest living in the Ganga River valley before this urbanization may be contained in the sacred Aranyakas (forest books) of the Vedas.

Exactly when the Upanishads were composed is not known. Modern historians date some of the Upanishads to be from 7,000 to 5,000 BCE (13). In general the composition of the Upanishads of the Vedas is said to belong to the second millennium BCE (7).

Following the close of the Upanishadic period further development of the doctrines about reincarnation, karma, and spiritual liberation resulted in the development of the six philosophical systems. The six philosophical systems that are based on the Vedas and developed by six sages are Nyaya, Vaisheshika, Samkhya, Yoga, Purva Mimamsa, and Uttara Mimamsa. This period ensued into the 'historical' times and eventually to the well-established dates for Gautama the Buddha (563 BCE to 483 BCE), founder of Buddhism, and Mahavira (540 BCE to 468 BCE) the founder of Jainism (7).

## THE SACRED HINDU SCRIPTURES

The word scripture generally means a handwritten sacred or religious document. It is the scripture that spells out the spiritual goal and the path to reach it. A scripture is generally considered as an authority in regulating human behavior, primarily for leading a religious life (13).

Hinduism is unique in the sense that, not only it is the most ancient continuously practiced religion, but also has the most amount of sacred material than any other religion (12).

The sacred Hindu scriptures are placed into three categories. Shruti, Smriti, and a subsidiary category.

**Shruti** means what is heard. Shruti contain the ever present divine revelations. Shruti scriptures are the Vedas which consist of the Samhita parts of Rigveda, Yajurveda, Samaveda, and Atharvaveda, and the appendages of the Vedas, namely, Brahmanas, Aranyakas, and the Upanishads. Shruti texts are the most sacred Hindu scriptures (11, 12, and 13).

**Smriti** means what is remembered. The scriptures belonging to smriti category have secondary authority only; the Shruti/Veda scriptures are the final authority (12). There is a multitude of smriti texts. The main scriptures that come under smriti texts are: The two great epics Ramayana and Mahabharata (Bhagavad-Gita is part of Mahabharata), the Puranas, and Dharma Shastras. Dharma-shastras are the law books; the most famous one is the Manu-smriti.

The subsidiary category includes Darshanas, Tantras and Shivāgamas (12). Darshanas are the six philosophical systems which are based on the Vedas and developed by six sages (11, 12). They are Nyaya, Vaisheshika, Samkhya, Yoga, Purva Mimamsa, and Uttara Mimamsa. The Darshana scriptures are called Dharma-sutras. The most famous of the sutras is the Brahma-sutras. Another set of scriptures, parallel to the Vedic scriptures, is called Tantra. The Tantric literature mainly consists that of Shaktism. Shivāgamas are the basic scriptures of the Shaivas.

## VEDA

The word 'Veda' means 'knowledge' or 'wisdom'. The Vedas are the records of revealed wisdom that have been faithfully passed down orally/verbally over thousands of years. They are the largest body of sacred literature surviving from the ancient world, and are the most impressive literary achievement of antiquity. The ability to preserve this comprehensive literature against the ravages of time is an incredible achievement (7).

The Hindu religious tradition has accorded the Veda the highest place, and as such, it is revered as the basic scripture of Hinduism (13). The Veda consists of collection of hymns (hymnodies) called Samhita *(Saṁhitā)*. The Samhita is the main part of the Veda, and it means that which has been collected and arranged in the form of mantra (11). Mantra is that which cultivates deep thought, and that which develops the mind. Mantras are sacred utterances which are repeated in various ways to direct the mental energies toward higher realities, especially to the 'One' (7). Mantra is a sacred syllable, word, phrase, poem or prose-text upon which one meditates by chanting repeatedly, either silently or aloud, so that the vibrations created again and again result in one's own well-being and the general well-being of others (11). The simplest and the most important mantra is 'Om'. Mantras are the expressions of the envisioned Divine Truths.

The mantras of the Vedas were revealed to various sages at different periods of time. It is said that the Rishis *(Ṛṣis)* cognized the mantras already in existence and made them known to the world (11). According to one calculation, the number of Vedic Rishis exceeds 800 (13). Consequently the style of language, grammar, ideas, as well as the historic and cultural factors vary widely (13).

Vedas, in all, are generally considered to have two portions. The first part is the portion dealing with action or rituals with the belief that Moksha (salvation/liberation) can be obtained through the right performance of rituals as enjoined by the Vedas. And the second part comes at the end of the Vedas dealing with knowledge that is said to be the quintessence of the Vedas (11). These two parts are considered to be complementary rather than contradictory to one another.

Veda, as the name implies, is informative – it supplies the information regarding the 'unknown'. It does not compel anyone to do anything; it simply prescribes means for attainment of desired results and avoidance of untoward effects (13). It has no barriers of race, creed or religion; it is universal and eternal (11). Veda does not state 'this is the only way' or 'this is the only God'. It makes it clear that any good religious path with faith and loyalty, and worship of any Divinity in whatever way, will lead to the true goal (11).

## Metric Composition

The Veda mantras were 'put-together' along with the Vedic Sanskrit language which has a wide range for plays on words and double meanings (10). The ancient sages painstakingly composed each hymn with rigorous standards of metric composition along with the 'perfected' Sanskrit language so that these poetic forms would be remembered, more so than the prose form, and transmitted verbally/orally, error-free, in posterity over thousands of years.

The Vedic hymns show considerable poetic sophistication and spiritual depth (7). There are about 19 or so distinct metres of composition, of which about 7 are frequently used.

There are rules as to how many lines/feet (pāda) are to be in each stanza, and how many syllables are to be in each line. The most common metre that appears in the Vedas has four lines. Name of the metre depends on the number of syllables in each line.

The *anushtup* with four lines and eight syllables in each to a total of 32 syllables is the most common metre.

The *gāyatrī* metre has four lines with six syllables in each to a total of 24 syllables, but, more commonly the gāyatri metre has three lines with eight syllables in each to the same total of 24 syllables, and this is called the *tripāda-gāyatri*. The famous Gāyatri Mantra which is named after the gāyatri metre itself has three lines with eight syllables in each line.

There are many other types of metrical compositions in the Vedas. If there are nine syllables in each of the four lines to a total of 36 syllables, then it is called *brihatee* meter. If there are ten syllables, then it is *pangti* metre. *Trishtup* metre has eleven syllables in each line to a total of 44 syllables. *Jagati* metre has twelve syllables in each of the four lines. (11).

When one line has a different number of syllables than the other, then it is called *vishama* which means not equal. If all the lines have different number of syllables in them, then it is said to be called *vishama vritta.* (11).

## Veda Vyāsa

In course of time a need arose to compile and record the Vedas. A sage by name Krishṇa Dvaipayana, now revered as the

Veda Vyāsa, meaning 'Veda Compiler', collected the Vedic hymns and arranged them into four Veda formats. All the hymns used by the Hotṛ-priest to invite the various divinities to the sacrificial ceremony became the Rigveda. All the worship related parts of the Vedas, useful to the Adhvaryu-priest, the chief executor of the sacrificial rites, formed the Yajurveda. Collection of all the musical chants, especially those associated with the Soma group of sacrifices, and to be sung by the Udgātṛ-priest (the singer), was named the Sāmaveda. The rest, a sort of miscellaneous appendix and addenda, assigned to the Brahma-priest who is considered as the supervisor over the whole sacrificial process, became the Atharvaveda (13).

It is generally believed that Veda Vyāsa classified the Vedas as above, more than 5,000 years ago (11). Furthermore, Vyāsa taught the Vedas to his four chief disciples, and assigned one each of the Vedas to them to be transmitted over the generations. Paila was assigned Rigveda, Vaiśampāyana the Yajurveda, Jaimini the Sāmaveda, and Samantu the Atharvaveda.

When Veda Vyāsa compiled the four Vedas, he entrusted one of his four chief disciples, sage Vaiśampāyana, to preserve the Yajurveda for posterity. This was the original version of the Yajurveda which is mostly in prose form. Vaiśampāyana taught this Veda to his many disciples including his chief disciple Yājñavalkya who in turn was supposed to do the same. However, it appears that Yājñavalkya had his own revelations in the form of a new version of Yajurveda named Shukla (white/bright) Yajurveda which is completely in hymn form. Hence, the original version, in retrospect was named Krishna (black/dark) Yajurveda.

The Veda Samhitas served as the foundation for the later additions to each in the form of Brahmanas (ritual texts), Aranyakas (ritual and meditational texts for forest dwelling ascetics), and the Upanishads (the esoteric texts).

Rigveda refers only to Rigveda Samhita; this is because the Brahmanas, Aranyakas and Upanishads attached to the Rigveda have their own separate names.

The Samhitas, in course of time, branched off to form about 1180 saakhas or recensions. A recension is a critical revision with intent to establish a definitive text. Each recension branch meant specialization by one group of scholars. The origin of these recensions is probably because the four principal disciples of Veda Vyāsa entrusted to preserve the Vedas in posterity, had several disciples of their own, and they and their successors might have done some readjustment of the Vedic mantras to suit the needs of the times (13). Very many of the recensions have been lost.

### Brāhmaṇa

The name of a specific Veda refers only to the Samhita; for example Rigveda refers only to the Rigveda Samhita. The Brāhmaṇas associated with the Vedas are explanatory scriptures which also are deemed to be revealed knowledge. Brahmanas come under the first part of the Vedas dealing with action or rituals with the belief that Moksha (salvation/liberation) can be obtained through the right performance of rituals as enjoined by the Vedas. Brahmana serves as a guidebook in the proper interpretation and use of the mantras supplied by the Samhitas. It is said that Samhita has the mantras, and all that is not mantra is Brahmana.

The Brahmana describes the minute details of sacrificial ceremonies, explaining their origin and hidden meaning, and illustrating their value and potency. Brahmana is considered as an attachment to the Samhita of the Veda. The two parts are clearly separated except in some prose part of the Yajurveda (Krishna Yajurveda, not Shukla Yajurveda) where, at times, the Brahmana is conjoined with the Samhita. Brahmana lists the Vedic rituals to be performed, and explains how they are to be performed. As the Vedic rituals grew more and more complex, the step by step home-based Vedic religious practice was taken over by priests who made the sacrifices even more elaborate (10). It is said that the Brahmana scriptures are perhaps less understood and less appreciated by modern scholars, than the Vedas themselves (10).

## Āraṇyaka

Āraṇyaka is a sacred text similar to the Brahmana, but intended for the forest dwellers who having fulfilled their householder duties, live in solitude in the forest. The focus is on certain powerful rites that lead to ritual purity followed by awakening of mystical powers. The symbolic and spiritual aspects of sacrifices are meditated upon; the meditation taking the place of the performance of sacrifices. Aranyakas also contain a number of meditational and devotional teachings similar to the Upanishads, and they stand midway between Brahmanas and Upanishads in form and spirit (10).

## Upanishad

Upa-ni-sada means 'to sit beside'. It is what is taught to a seeker who sits by the side. Upanishads are personalized instructions to those who are fit to receive them. The general thrust of the teachings is towards non-dualism – ultimately, all things are one, and that the innermost essence of the human being is the very same essence that underlies the universe at large (7). Upanishads are the best known aspects of the Vedic literature. They not only come at the end of the textual presentation of the Vedas, but also contain the ultimate goal of the realization of the end-product of the Vedas.

## Mahāvākyas

Each of the Vedas has many great sayings or great passages known as Mahāvākyas. But four, one from each Veda, are important, very thought provoking, and powerful. They are contained in the knowledge part of the Vedas in the four Upanishads.

In Aitareya Upanishad of Rigveda, it is said *'Prajñānam Brahma'* meaning that exalted actual experience alone is Brahman (Supreme knowledge is Brahman). In Bṛhadāraṇyaka Upanishad of Shukla Yajurveda *'aham brahmasmi'* means 'I am Brahman'. In Chāndogya Upanishad of Sāmaveda *'tattvamasi (tat-tvam-asi)'* means 'that thou art' or 'you are that (you are Ātman)'. In the Māṇḍūkya Upanishad of Atharvaveda *'ayamātma brahma'* means 'This Ātman is Brahman' (11).

These great sayings – **Supreme knowledge is Brahman, I am Brahman, You are Ātman, and This Ātman is Brahman** - clearly state the philosophy of non-dualism (Monism) – the individual Self and the Universal Self is one and the same, and that there is only one Absolute Reality.

## CHANTING THE VEDA

Veda in ancient Sanskrit which previously was purely an oral literature, has been faithfully passed down orally/verbally over thousands of years. The ability to preserve this comprehensive literature against the ravages of time is an incredible achievement (7). Vedas consist of collection of hymns called mantras. In order to preserve the purity of the Veda mantras, in addition to verbally transmitting the Vedic hymns, the methods of chanting and the rules of pronunciation had to be transmitted over generations.

The Veda mantras had to be chanted exactly, so as to produce the same perfect vibrations and sounds every time. Error-free chanting was of prime importance. It was believed that error-free chanting of the mantras, even chanting a single mantra correctly, was beneficial to the chanter whether the person understood the meaning of the mantra or not. Accordingly, in the early times, the ancient sages devised a unique chanting system that consisted of various chanting modes to help pronounce the mantras correctly. Each mantra, one at a time, had to be chanted in various patterns and combinations.

First is to recite one mantra at a time in full (*Vākya Pāṭha*). Vakya means a sentence.

Mantra in a sentence has some words joined together to form compounded words. Some sounds of syllables and words change depending on their environment, particularly at the junction (sandhi) of the words. Rules of these changes are called sandhi rules. The main aim of reciting in this mode is to make no mistake in the original meaning and sound pattern of the mantra. This Patha is considered as a natural lesson because the words of the mantra occur in a natural normal sequence during recitation (11).

Next is reciting the same mantra, word by word (*Pada Pāṭha*), without conjoining the words, and not stringing the words as above. Pada means word. Here the pronunciations of individual words that had been conjoined before according to the sandhi rules revert back to their own individual sound pattern. For example, Sat (which means eternal existence, being), Chit (which means consciousness, knowledge), and Ānanda (which means infinite bliss), are pronounced as such individually - Sat, Chit, and Ānanda - in Pada Patha. When these three words are put together, they become Sacchidānanda. Note that 't' in Sat changes to 'ch', and 't' in Chit changes to 'd'. Pada Patha is also considered as a natural lesson because the words of the mantra occur in a normal sequence despite the change in the pronunciation (11).

Then it gets more complicated. *Krama Pāṭha* is practiced after Pada Patha. In this method of chanting, the first word is joined with the second, the second word with the third, and the third with the fourth and so on. This practice lesson helps understand not only the individual word sounds, but also the modification that occurs with combination of words. The word sequencing here is 1-2; 2-3; 3-4; and so on. It is not a natural sequence of words as 1-2-3-4 and on. The word sequence is considered not-natural or artificial. There are more non-natural Pathas (11).

*Jata Pāṭha* is recited next. Here the sequence of two words is different. First and second words are recited together, then the two words are recited in a reverse order, and then they are recited again in the right order. This type of sequencing is continued onwards. Thus the order of words is 1-2-2-1-1-2; 2-3-3-2-2-3; and so on. In *Shikha Pāṭha*, three word combinations, instead of two, are recited. The other lessons, *Rekha, Dhvaja, Danda, Ratha, Ghana,* etc. are even more complex chanting methods (11).

Although this system of chanting is so complex, the interested individuals were encouraged to learn more difficult methods of recitation, as the benefit of chanting more complex methods correctly, was said to be proportionately higher than that of the easier ones. It appears that this complex system of chanting methods was helpful in preserving the Veda mantras in a pure form. These lessons focused mainly on the error-free chanting, and not on understanding the meaning of the Veda mantras. More important safeguards called Vedāngas (limbs of the Vedas) were devised by the ancient seers, not only for error-free chanting, but also to understand the wisdom of the Vedas.

## SANSKRIT SCRIPT

Script is a written form of language. Rigveda, the most ancient of all compositions, was fashioned along with the old Vedic Sanskrit language which was purely an oral literature then. Beginning of this period is generally considered to be around 10,000 BCE (13). The Vedic seers have stated (page xv of reference 9) that:

*'Samskritam (Sanskrit) is the name of a scientifically standardized language evolved by the seers out of the primitive articulate speech by subjecting it to grammatical analyses'.*

In this regard references in the Vedas themselves are given: Rigveda I.164.50 and X.90.16, Krishna Yajurveda III.5.11, Shukla Yajurveda 31.16, and Atharvaveda VII.5.1.

*'The scholars (here it says devas) carried out the operation/yajna (said to mean composition of hymns); these were their first duties/dharma'.*

The Vedas in ancient Sanskrit have been faithfully passed down orally/verbally over thousands of years. The presence of this strong oral tradition does not preclude ancient written records. It seems that without a script, the Vedic poets would have found it exceedingly difficult to meet rigorous standards of Sanskrit metric composition; the poets knew more than fifteen distinct metres of composition (7). Furthermore, Shukla Yajurveda XVII.2 says (16, 17):

*'O Agni, may these bricks be mine own kine; one, and ten, and ten tens, a hundred, and ten hundreds, a thousand, and ten thousand a myriad, and a hundred thousand, and a million, and a hundred million, and an ocean middle and end, and a hundred thousand millions, and a billion'.*

It is stated that counting involving such large numbers without some form of written annotation is impossible (7). Also, it is to be noted that ancient people of India knew such notation of large numbers thousands of years ago. The concept of one million did not become common in the west until the nineteenth century CE (AD) (7). Furthermore, the geometric design of the Vedic fire-altar involved mathematical calculation that could not possibly be done in the mind alone; there had to be some sort of writing involved (7). The ancient seers not only had the ability to write numbers, but also knew how to write literature.

Evidences of writing can be inferred from the Vedas themselves: Rigveda X.62.7 uses the term '*ashṭa-karṇyah*' meaning 'eight-marked ears' and refers to cattle – cattle that had their ears marked with numeral eight. Atharvaveda XIX.72.1 says that *'Veda is to be placed back in the chest from where it was taken',* implying that there was a written form of the Veda then (18). Writing might have been executed on perishable material such as palm leaves, and birch bark or some other form of wood.

**In India, the earliest form of available writing has been traced as far back as 3,300 BCE.** Archeological findings from Mohenjo-Daro, Harappa and other sites reveal about 4,200 objects that have inscriptions on them. They are mainly carvings on seals, small pieces of soft-stone, and a few copper tablets. They reveal a surprisingly mature system of writing. There are about 400 different signs including numerals. The longest text is twenty-six signs long, with an average length of five signs (7).

Because of the false theory of 'Aryan Invasion of India' which had claimed that there was no Sanskrit or Veda prior to the so called invasion around 1,500 BCE, it had been thought that the above Indus-valley script was probably related to old form of Tamil script, thus making deciphering of the script enigmatic. But now that the theory has been disproven and thus defunct, the script has been compared to Sanskrit language and the later Brahmi script. This comparison has revealed that the Indus-Sarasvati script of 3,300 BCE evolved into the Brahmi script of 300 BCE (7, 19).

Brahmi stands for Goddess Sarasvati the Goddess of learning. Brahmi script was used by Emperor Ashoka, also known as Ashoka the Great who ruled India from 268 BCE to 232 BCE, to inscribe his edicts on stone pillars that are found all over India. Current evidence clearly shows that Brahmi script is derived from the Indus-Sarasvati script (7, 19).

Scripts of all the modern languages of India have originated from the Brahmi script. From Brahmi, two prominent branches of scripts developed: The present-day Sanskrit script called the Devanagari script and the scripts of the North Indian languages evolved from one branch; and the other branch in South India, evolved into the languages of South India (10, 19).

**It is to be noted that all the South Indian and all the North Indian languages, including their scripts, evolved from Sanskrit.**

*Om*

## REFERENCES

1. The Rig Veda. Complete. Translated by Ralph T. H, Griffith. Republished 2008 by Forgotten Books.

2. OUT OF EDEN. The peopling of the world. Stephen Oppenheimer. Constable & Robinson Ltd. 3 the Lanchesters, 162 Fulham Palace Road, London W6 9ER, UK. Revised paperback edition 2004

3. CHANDOGYA UPANISHAD by Swami Swahananda. Sri Ramakrishna Math, Mylapore, Chennai (Madras) 600 004, India. 2007

4. ISHAVASYOPANISHAD by Swami Sharvananda. Sri Ramakrishna Math, Madras 600 004, India. 2007

5. THE BHAGAVAD GITA with Sanskrit Text. Translated by Swami Chidbhavananda. Sri Ramakrishna Tapovanam, Tirupparaitturai, India. 1976

6. The Myth of the Aryan Invasion of India. David Frawley (Vamadeva Shastri). Voice of India, 2/18 Ansari Road, New Delhi-110 002, India. Third Enlarged Edition: June 2005

7. IN SEARCH OF THE CRADLE OF CIVILIZATION. New Light on Ancient India. Georg Feuerstein, Subhash Kak and David

Frawley. Motilal Banarsidass Publishers, Delhi, India. This Edition reproduced from Quest Books 2001 Edition.

8. History and Philosophy of Lingayat Religion. M. R. Sakhare. 1978 Karnataka University, Dharwad, Karnataka, India.

9. RIGVEDA SAMHITA according to the translation of H. H. Wilson, and Bhashya of Sayanacharya, volumes I through IV. Ravi Prakash Arya, K. L. Joshi. Primal Publications. Indica Books, D 40/18 Godowlia, Varanasi 221 001, India. 2002

10. GODS, SAGES AND KINGS. Vedic Secrets of Ancient Civilization, by David Frawley. Passage Press, Morison Publishing, P. O. Box 21713, Salt Lake City, Utah 84121, USA. 1991

11. The Vedas. Sri Chandrasekharendra Saraswati, Bhavan's Book University, Bharatiya Vidya Bhavan, Mumbai, India. Eighth Edition 2009.

12. The Essentials of Hinduism. A Comprehensive Overview of the World's Oldest Religion. Swami Bhaskarananda. 2002 by the Vedanta Society of Western Washington, Viveka Press, Seattle, WA 98102, USA.

13. Holy Scriptures. A Symposium on the Great Scriptures of the World. Sri Ramakrishna Math, Mylapore, Madras, India.

14. The World's Last Mysteries. The Reader's Digest Association, Inc., Pleasantville, New York. Seventh Printing. March 1982

15. BRAHMA-SUTRAS. According to Shri Shankara. Swami Vireswarananda. Advaita Ashrama, 5 Dehi Entally Road, Kolkata, India. Ninth Impression, April 2005

16. YAJURVEDA SAMHITA (SHUKLA), Sanskrit Text with English Translation by R. T. H. Griffith, Edited and revised with an introduction and exegical notes by Ravi Prakash Arya. Primal Publications India Books, D 40/18 Godowlia, Varanasi – 221 001 (UP), India. 2002

17. The Texts of the White Yajurveda Translated by Ralph T. H. Griffith. Republished 2008 by Forgotten Books.

18. ATHARVAVEDA SAMHITA, Sanskrit Text, English Translation, Notes & Index of Verses According to the Translation of W. D. Whitney and Bhashya of Sayanacharya, Edited and revised by K. L. Joshi. Primal Publications, Delhi, India. First Edition 2000

19. VEDIC GLOSSARY ON INDUS SEALS by Dr. N. Jha, edited by B. K. Jha, Ganga Kaveri Publishing House, D. 35/77, Jangamawadimath, Varanasi 221 001 India. 1996

Made in the USA
Middletown, DE
06 January 2021